WHAT PEOPLE ARE SAYING

"The reality of life is full of distractions, negative opinions from others, and false messages from the media. In *Creating Confidence*, Alana Andrews shares milestones from various experiences that have shaped her approach to life. Using personal stories from school, athletics, nutrition, friendship, family, and much more, Alana helps readers identify self-worth using various strategies to "stay positive." This is a must read for adolescent children, teenagers, parents, educators, and anyone in need of inspiration!"

Dave Shaffer,
Principal, River Bend Middle School

"In this book, Ms. Andrews gives us an intimate look into her personal beliefs and experiences. Her positivity is genuine and will serve as a source of inspiration to all young people. Confidence exudes in her written words, allowing her to become the maker of her destiny!"

Nahid Haidari,
M. Ed., Vice Principal, Potowmack Elementary School

"Creating Confidence infused with poise and power allows us to believe in the seemingly impossible. Andrews inspires us to reflect upon our own internal greatness through the lens of family and friends, promoting strength from within through the support of others. Her combination of introspection, daily routine, and self-reliance provides a recipe for continuous growth and achievement."

Nick Cottone,
Principal, Seneca Ridge Middle School

PREVIOUSLY
BY
ALANA ANDREWS

Timeless...Poetry from the Soul of a Teen's Heart

CREATING CONFIDENCE

ALANA

ANDREWS

Forward Written
By

Carole Stizza, ACC, SSCS, SHRM-SCP

Speaker, Author, and Coach with Relevant Insight LLC

Contributing author in Compassion @ Work (2017) and

Coaches Wisdom-Vol.1 (2018)

ISBN-13: 978-1729533079

ISBN-10: 1729533078

I dedicate this book to my parents. Thank you for believing in me and building the confidence that you've always seen in me. I will give to others because of what you've always given to me.

Thank you.

As we express our gratitude, we must never forget that the highest appreciation is not to utter words but to live by them.

- John F. Kennedy

CONTENTS

FORWARD

Dear Adults

Ever since the education system opened, there has been and will continue to be, critical analysis of how children develop, how they behave, and what will become of us all when they move into the workforce, politics and beyond. I, myself, pondered how to be a better parent when I was rearing my kids to give them the best of me while letting them bloom into the best of them. Many parents will look at their children and wonder, have we done our best?

While I want to assure you that your best was what you delivered at that moment in time, there will always be more to learn, people to emulate in how they raised their child differently. There will be new perspectives that will make you wish you could turn back time and offer a little more.

There will also be a debate about what is the most influential factor in a child's success. Nature versus nurture – or a magic combination of both? Is it their natural gifts and strengths versus the skills taught and trained by others?

Regardless of your choices, few will deny that confidence is critical to persevering and succeeding. So, then we ponder, can confidence be taught and learned? Confidence is something many feels is simply gained by personal experience over time, and I can honestly say, I may have been one of those who thought the same way. That confidence building is a journey forged with a time requirement.

It wasn't until I started meeting extraordinary young people, like Alana Andrews, that made me wonder if how they were raised contributed to their unique qualities. Showing signs of such great confidence at a young age flew in the face of my idea of time requirements. What was unique about their personal journeys that gave them insights, characteristics, and qualities that propelled them farther, faster, and with more joy than the average teenager. Could they have just emerged with this light shining out of them or was it introduced?

If so, when should we all start to introduce and build confidence in our own kids, teenagers, college students, or employees? With employees, it starts from the time they come into the interview and ask the employer about what it takes to succeed when hired. They know to ask. Children do not - and yet they aspire to succeed with every new attempt to walk, talk, and share. They must be met with the acceptance and support required to understand how to persevere through failure and not fall apart.

I have studied this topic and have my own perspectives on how to build confidence at work. It is a critical part in building a career. And yet, few books offer insights into this topic from the perspective of the minds of our youth. Alana offers a glimpse into the future of our workforce through her perspectives that will shape our tomorrow.

This book provides unique proof that our youth today will be great leaders tomorrow - and Alana Andrews will be leading the pack! The pages of this book provide an amazing look inside the mind, life, and wonderful confidence of Alana Andrews.

At the ripe age of 14, I can guarantee that this young phenom will make you think twice about how you think, act, and reflect on your own confidence journey, and how you build the confidence of others you touch, and how you regard raising your own children and grandchildren.

While this is not a parenting book – it should be. This is a book that every parent – young and old – should read to understand their part in instilling the confidence in those they love.

If I had had access to Alana's book, I could honestly admit that my own children's journey with confidence may have been more successful than the one we were able to provide at the time. We will never know, of course, as my own kids are adults now with lives of their own and thriving – possibly despite our parenting.

This may be why Grandparents enjoy their grandchildren more than when they raised their own kids. They get a 'do-over' after accumulating more knowledge. I know that I feel this way and I must admit, after meeting and working with Alana, and now reading her book, I'm humbled to realize I could have offered more to my own kids in building their confidence.

This is also a book that every young teenager should read to put in place the thinking they need to evaluate who they want to be, and how they want to present themselves to the world, no apologies needed! If you are wondering what our future holds, look no further than the confidence of this amazing, yet young, talented Alana Andrews!

Carole Stizza, ACC, SSCS, SHRM-SCP
Speaker, Author, and Coach with Relevant Insight LLC
Contributing author in Compassion @ Work (2017)
and Coaches Wisdom-Vol.1 (2018)

Dear Future Adults,

Enjoy this book! Not because it is about Alana, but because it is about what she experienced that has allowed her to reflect on her journey and how she has gained the confidence to think differently about the world she needs to see positively change.

Alana is unique as an individual – yes! And yet, she is not unique as a teenager with a great mind – she had a deep need to be like others despite a scary health issue – and she set out to see if she could solve that problem. All future adults like you are amazing at solving problems, it just takes the idea and the confidence to see that idea land somewhere useful. Alana's first idea was not how the final idea will come into the world, yet it had to start somewhere that made sense for her. I am eternally grateful that I got to be a part of her beginning.

It is a fascinating privilege for professionals, like me, who are older than yourself, with different experiences, to get to see how brilliant your minds are at your age. It allows us to remember the problems we wanted to see solved when we were the same age. I hope this book inspires you to offer one of your solutions to the world, wherever you are. Find someone who will listen to you and connect you to someone in business that can support your idea moving forward. It may not happen right away. With confidence, you can persevere. With perseverance, comes success. Learn, like Alana, that NO from one person, is not NO from every person.

I get to meet people on a regular basis who have started a business simply by matching a solution to a need. Once they figured out how to offer and market that solution, they were in business, and it didn't have to start off fancy. Just the basics work. Most great ideas are not fancy – they just work. Alana's idea is a great example of that.

Her confidence is a magic ingredient.

So, enjoy reading through these pages. Each chapter brings forth the stories of how she is now able to step into the unknown adventures of offering a unique idea that solves a pain point that she has personally experienced. She now has the opportunity, grown out of taking an idea to investors, to market, manufacture, and beyond, to help serve a community of teenagers who may suffer, now or in the future, from a disease that is scary and who want solutions too.

Carole Stizza, ACC, SSCS, SHRM-SCP

Speaker, Author, and Coach with Relevant Insight LLC

Contributing author in Compassion @ Work (2017) and

Coaches Wisdom-Vol.1 (2018)

Creating Confidence

Because one believes in oneself, one doesn't try to convince others. Because one is content with oneself, one doesn't need others' approval. Because one accepts oneself, the whole world accepts him or her.

– Lao Tzu

For the past fourteen years, my parents have been planting seeds of confidence in me, and today, they are healthy roots that are not easily shaken by the negative opinions of what others may think. For a teenager, that's no easy feat, but it helps when you can understand that opinions are something that everyone has. It's up to you to decide if someone's opinion of you is in your best interest.

Knowing that you are empowered to put those unwanted opinions on a shelf like a returned item is empowering itself. My dad taught my brother and I how to play chess when we were six years old, and he's constantly reminding us that everything in life is a chess move and you must remember when to make the right move.

Sometimes you must sacrifice your knight on the chessboard. In other words, you must put yourself in the right position to win the game.

The time that he invested into teaching us how to play the game has so many benefits. I have acquired an overall view of life from the perspective of a teenager. I now understand that to navigate successfully through life, you must put yourself in the driver's seat, decide where you're going, and stay focused on getting there without distractions. Feeling good about myself is as natural as breathing.

My parents echo of encouragement has been continuously ringing in my ears, as they would say, "Alana, greatness lives in you." "You can do anything. "You're beautiful." Today, those words are alive with purpose, as my parents will look at me and ask, "Alana, what lives in you?" I instinctively tell them without thinking that greatness lives in me. And it does. It's something that I know without a doubt.

Confidence is a feeling of self-assurance arising from your appreciation of your abilities or qualities. Similarly, self-esteem is the opinion that you have of yourself. Having a healthy self-image, high confidence in yourself, and an excellent level of self-esteem are the factors that will affect the way that you may act, have success in school, see yourself in the mirror and in how you interact with others.

Having self-confidence may allow you to set high, yet realistic goals and will guide you to not back down from challenges. You'll be more inclined to make the best decisions. Also, you'll have the confidence to acknowledge your mistakes and know your boundaries.

Many generations have failed to pursue their dreams and wishes because their level of self-esteem can affect their decision-making process. Low self-esteem most commonly comes from a low self-image in one's appearance.

As said in a *Daily Mail* survey, one-fourth of girls aged between eleven and seventeen are brought down by pressure to look a certain way. Low self-esteem may have an enormous effect on the choice of a female's career. Also, young girls spend forty-two minutes a day trying to change the way they look by changing their clothes in the morning often, as well as spending time applying makeup. Many young girls have also said they would be happier if they were more physically attractive.

Being fourteen years old is exciting and filled with so many dreams. It's also filled with false realities of what the media says about how teenage girls should present themselves to the world. Some girls may compare themselves to others in every way. It's not uncommon to hear the way teens mentally put themselves down.

They'll sometimes comment on how they feel about themselves by saying they're ugly, they're too skinny, they're overweight, or they don't love themselves. They don't often see the good in who they are. They consistently compare themselves to others.

I can hear the echoes of my mom telling me that everyone is different. Everyone has unique qualities that adds value to others and the world. It can sometimes be challenging for a person to see their value. Instead of looking at the positive things about themselves, they'll tend to find the negative. Most of the time, it's all mental. If you see yourself as beautiful, then you'll feel beautiful. It works both ways. Like my mom always says, "at the end of the day, it's up to you because you have to decide which road you'll travel." When she's sharing those magical words of wisdom, which is quite often, I sometimes think to myself, wow, that's good stuff.

When you have self-confidence, it can help you believe in yourself and in your ability to achieve greatness. It goes a long way in so many areas of your life. For example, as a student, we are busy with our classes and the amount of work that each requires and there are many things that you can do to achieve success. However, you can know everything there is to know about a quiz, but if you don't believe that you are capable of succeeding, you can often decrease your chances of getting that A. This isn't the case for everyone. But I've walked down the halls of my school and have heard many students speak so much failure to their future exam and yet they haven't even taken the test. They'll say, "I just know I'm not going to do well." "I'm not going to make an A, this is too hard." If you adequately prepare for a test, you have the best chance of succeeding without the negative self-talk. If you've done your homework by studying and making the necessary preparation, you can know that you should do well. The greatest advice that I would share with any student is that when you believe that you'll succeed, you'll discover your abilities to achieve greatness.

During my eighth-grade year, I was challenged to take on the debates. Our teacher had told us that to raise our grade, we would have to show how our answers were correct if they were marked wrong. I don't know why, but I was excited about the challenge. During my excitement, I also began to feel somewhat nervous, as I wasn't clear how it would all play out. I had prepared notes the night before proving that my answers were correct. This gave me confidence early on only because I knew my content before going into the debate.

The day had finally arrived, and my heart was pounding more and more as my turn was getting closer. I faced my nerves and took on the challenge because I felt confident in knowing that I knew the material. It was that confidence that I had that carried me on to earn several additional points for my grade. I knew within myself that I could and would achieve my goal.

From that experience, I learned that when you're confident in your work, it generates a specific emotion that enables you to feel empowered to achieve a goal. I felt empowered to take on the challenge of the debate, and if I were not prepared, I would have missed out on the experience of succeeding in the face of fear.

That's so powerful because that experience is one that I will carry as a milestone on my path in life.

As I grow and prepare for new experiences in high school and college, my eyes continue to open to see, and my mind opens for me to understand the process that my parents used in planting the seeds of self-confidence in me. When you become rooted in who you are, it's the same as being grounded in your beliefs. I believed that if I put in the work by studying and preparing for the challenge of the debates, I would succeed. And you know what? I did.

I always remind myself that although I may have experienced some success in life, it hasn't been a journey that I've taken by myself, nor is it a road that I choose to be on alone. If it weren't for my parents love and desire for me to learn how to believe in myself, I wouldn't have the experiences that I'm able to share with the you.

Creating confidence is a journey that is filled with the roadblocks of fear, disappointment, challenges, and setbacks. Notice that I didn't say failure. My father taught me that failure exists only when you quit. I'm not a quitter because I believe too much in myself and want to keep moving forward.

I know that some may say that it sounds easier than it really is. And for some, that may be true. As a teenager transitioning into high school, I've seen a lot of what goes on with other teens. When their parents aren't very supportive, it can be devasting and hurtful. We want so much for our parents to believe in us, and their approval matters the most. What some parents may not realize is that their words can be harrowing and sharp. It can cut the core of a teen's self-confidence.

Some students are saved by their teachers' belief in them and their ability to be great. It doesn't matter who's inspiring you to believe in yourself. If you find there's no one to believe in you, it's okay because you can become your inspiration.

There are several ways that you can create confidence in yourself.

- Listen to music that inspires you to do good. Be mindful of the lyrics. The words could hurt your purpose for building a positive mind-set and your self-confidence. Some songs sound good, but the words can make you feel bad about yourself and others.

- Develop friendships with your peers that are confident about school, their life, and themselves. Someone once said that "birds of a feather flock together." That's true. When you surround yourself with confident people, you begin to feel confident as well. When you surround yourself with people that are doing positive things, you'll find yourself doing the same thing.

- Think about the best outcome in a negative situation. For example, when the debates in class challenged me, I could have looked at that as an opportunity to increase my grade, or I could have seen it as an opportunity to complain about why we had to debate in front of our entire class. I decided to take the challenge because things could only get better when you try. The same amount of energy that you spend complaining is the same energy that you can give to working toward achieving a goal.

- Journal your thoughts. I've found that when I journal, it allows me to carry my thoughts to so many different places. I'm able to release stress and pressure because I'm releasing it on paper. Plus, you've created an opportunity to see what you're feeling. It can be a game changer. Trust me, it works.

- Talk to your parents, guardian, teacher, counselor, school administrative staff, or someone who understands what it's like to be a student. They've been where you're going. They are here to help and more importantly, to listen with an understanding heart. Having an adult to listen and understand what you're feeling can make the difference in how you think about a situation. It can also be the deciding factor when you are faced with a big decision.

Learn to love yourself. Value yourself and all the beautiful things that make you unique. If your friends continuously point out how funny your laugh is, then embrace the fact that you're making them smile. If someone points out that you walk funny, then celebrate that once again you've managed to add laughter to the world.

Another word of advice from my mom is when she says "Everyone is on the path to believing in themselves. We won't ever arrive at the destination because as humans, we consistently have opportunities to discover new and exciting things about ourselves." Wow, that's good stuff.

Remember the point that I made earlier about other opinions? Everybody has one. It's up to you to decide if it's in your best interests to keep it. You must know that you are empowered to put it on the shelf like a returned item.

Creating confidence is a decision to make, and the journey that you take will be on a path that will take you to so many places. It doesn't matter where you start, but if you begin, you'll get there.

It Doesn't Matter

The best way to predict the future is to invent it.

– Alan Kay

I magine what it's like at seven years old. You don't look like your peers. Your hair is different because it's tight and curly, whereas most of your peers' hair is long and straight. Your skin is different, your smile is different, and most importantly, your weight is different. That was me, Alana Andrews. It was apparent that I was unique, or different, as some would see it.

At that age, we are just curious kids with a bucket of questions for anyone who appeared to know the answers. The questions that were always asked of me was about my hair. "Alana, why is your hair so curly?" or "Alana, may I touch your hair? Wow, it feels like cotton."

That was my introduction to self-awareness. Up until then, I was just a little girl with eyes as big as the sun. My biggest concern was how much longer I could stay outside and play with my friends. I didn't care much about anything else.

The one thing that my parents taught me at an early age was to love everything about being me. Many people have asked me how I created an actual love for myself. Being able to love myself came from my parents loving me. But you can develop a genuine love for yourself by enjoying and appreciating the essence of just being you.

My parents showed me love in how patient they were with me when I wanted to learn how to ride my bike, make my sandwiches, and wrap my gifts. Everything was always positive. In return, I always felt good about myself. I felt valuable and essential to them. Whenever I had something to say, they gave me the attention that I needed to talk as they intensely listened. They always made me feel important by reassuring me that what I said mattered. Little did I know that each day my confidence was building a wall of strength that would be there for me throughout the years as a protector, leader, guide, and friend.

I'm always ready to listen to my parents' stories about the path they carved out for me as they intentionally worked consistently on the development of my self-confidence. I will never forget how my mother would say that there was nothing wrong with me and my siblings. Although when my brother, Shang decided to give me a haircut in his make-believe barbershop, Mom wasn't too happy, and she let us know that what we did was terrible, but she continuously emphasized that we were good kids. I didn't understand what that meant, but I do recall how good it made me feel.

I felt an enormous love from her whenever I made a mistake, for she had a way of making me think that I needed to think twice about repeating something that wasn't too pleasing to her. But she kept showing me love by hugging me, kissing me, and playing with me on a consistent basis.

Those hugs and kisses don't stop, even when you're in middle-school. I remember when my mom chaperoned my 6th grade class fieldtrip to the zoo in Washington, DC. In the middle of nowhere, she gave me an enormous hug and kiss right in front of our group. Although I felt embarrassed as most teenagers do, I also felt on top of the world because her actions showed me that I mattered at home, at school, and in public. I felt a great amount of self-worth that day because she not only spent the day with me and hundreds of 6th graders, but she expressed her love for me in front of them.

Today, my mother continues to tell us that greatness is in each of us.

I've always been curious as to why my parents placed so much emphasis on ensuring that my siblings and I were prepared with the confidence needed for school, our dreams, and life itself. They always told me that when you have faith, it becomes the driving force that will get you through life. The yes that you give to yourself is more powerful than a thousand noes.

Having self-confidence is a way of life for some. It's a belief that you develop within yourself of knowing that you can dream any dream and work hard to reach any goals that you may desire. But, to maintain that mind-set, you must be consciously aware of what goes in your mind because it can create positive or negative thoughts. I've always leaned toward the positive side of things, for it makes me feel good when I do. I will always credit my parents for creating an environment of positivity around me.

I had so many fun memories of being in preschool. One of which was during the mornings when my mom would drive my brother Shang and I to school. She would play the most uplifting music for us to sing and dance all the way to our class. Those rides seem so short because we would have such an amazing time singing. Shang and I would sit in the back seat and dance while we kept the most gigantic smiles glistening across our small faces. The feeling of happiness didn't end when we arrived. When we got out of the car, we would jump and sing as if no one was around. At that age, you don't seem to care too much about whose watching you when you're in the middle of having the best time of your life. For us, we were having the best time of our lives. Those songs prepared us for the day ahead. It was the best feeling ever. This happened every single day without fail. My parents have been consistent in everything that they've ever done as they worked to build our self-confidence.

When I began elementary school, my brother and I would wake up each morning to hear songs like "It Doesn't Matter," "Beautiful Day," "Lovely Day," and the list goes on. My mom would even play motivational speeches like "I Am A Champion."

All of this took place before, during, and after breakfast. Before my brother and I were ready to leave for school, we felt empowered and equipped with the code of honor that was filled with words of wisdom, confidence, and life. My mother would ask, "Do you have your coat of confidence on for the day?" We would reply, "Yes, we're ready." And she would say, "Have the BEST DAY EVER!!!!" and we did.

It has been several years since that first car ride to preschool, and yet today, I subconsciously wake up in the mornings to play some of the same songs. I have learned to empower myself. Sometimes I'll ask my mom why she would inspire us so much with the positive music and speeches in the morning. She referred to a Chinese proverb, "Give a man a fish, and you feed him for a day. Teach a man to fish, and you feed him for a lifetime." My aha moment was when I finally realized that she was teaching us how to empower ourselves.

Today, I consciously follow that same model. I make sure that whatever I watch on my computer or listen to reflects positive feelings. The music, the lyrics, the motivational speeches have all been a part of developing my self-confidence. Waking up each morning and hearing songs that are designed to inspire you, over a period of time becomes a part of your being.

When I was in elementary school, I didn't see many students that looked like me or had hair like me. To my peers, my hair seemed like a fluffy cotton ball that was so soft when touched. One day a classmate asked me why my hair was so curly. More importantly, my classmate wanted to know why my hair looked different than most of the other students. At that age, you are inquisitive and innocent. I just remember saying that my mom said that we're all different and being different makes each of us unique.

One day during the first grade, I arrived home to share with my mom my day, and I told her that the questions from my classmates began to feel a little uncomfortable. I just didn't understand why it drew so much of their attention. She sat down to explain to me how being unique is powerful and it sets me apart for being average. She told me that everyone is unique with unique gifts, talents, and qualities.

So, we decided to create a song about being okay with just being you. We chose to do so because we felt it would allow me to share how I feel inside, and it could help others embrace their hair, skin color, just themselves.

"It Doesn't Matter" was written and produced in 2011. My siblings and I, along with my parents, worked together to create a home video for the song. We went into a studio to produce the music and after a short period of time, my first music CD was available on iTunes. I felt so empowered, confident and proud. From that point on, I began to feel even more proud to have short and curly hair.

My hair may never be a long as some, and it may never be as short as others. But none of that matters, for it will never define who I am. I am Alana Andrews, smart, powerful, fearless, innovative, beautiful, intelligent, funny, loyal, and committed to being the best me that I can be.

"It Doesn't Matter" became the first project of the So Positive brand, that would soon become So Positive, LLC. I'm so proud that it's still available on iTunes. When I look back on it today, I think to myself how funny the video was and about the sound quality of the music. But we did it. My family supported me and helped to build my self-confidence in accepting my hair and everything else that makes me young, beautiful, and unique.

My favorite line in the song says:

It doesn't matter if they make

fun of me,

It doesn't matter because I know what I can be.

It doesn't matter even if I fall,

Cause inside of me, I'm ten feet tall.

Wow. Every time I hear those words, I feel so empowered. It doesn't matter if you're three, four, or even five feet tall. What matters is how you feel inside. Life happens and people are human, which means we're all subject to human error. That's why it's important to know who you are and what you love about life and yourself.

People will make fun of you. I don't believe that anyone is exempt from that reality. Life makes fun of us. Have you ever gone for a walk along a trail and seen a piece of a tree limb on the ground? That has happened to me a few times. However, there have been times when that tree limb looked like a snake, and for a brief second, I instinctively jump out of fear, only to realize that my mind was playing tricks on me. I often just laugh at myself when that happens.

When you can find a way to laugh at yourself, it makes it easier to get through the times when life seems to challenge us the most.

Girls SO Positive

Don't wait until everything is just right. It will never be perfect. There will always be challenges, obstacles, and less-than-perfect conditions. So what? Get started now. With each step you take, you will grow stronger and stronger, more and more skilled, more and more self-confident and more and more successful.

– Mark Victor

I Will never forget the summer of 2013. I was looking forward to being in the fourth grade. All the kids in my neighborhood and I waited each day patiently for the *big* letter to arrive in the mail

The *big* letter was the announcement of who our new teacher would be. With my fingers crossed in anticipation and excitement. I wanted to have Mrs. Oberlander. Not only was she my brother Shang's teacher, but she also had an enormous passion for teaching through music. I knew that she had a big, brown, and beautiful guitar in her classroom.

Moreover, I also knew that she made learning about the history of Virginia musically memorable. The day arrived and... *yes*! Mrs. Oberlander was my fourth-grade teacher. I was so thrilled with joy and wonder.

Although it felt as if we spent the whole summer waiting for the big announcement, my mom and I were also busy working on creating my new YouTube talk show. When you're about to enter the fourth grade, there seem to be so many things to talk about with your friends. It was a time when I began to realize that girls my age were starting to group themselves into cliques. It became important what you were wearing and how you looked. I wanted to remain friends with everyone, and I wanted to create a place for girls like me to talk about the things that interest them the most.

After sharing my thoughts with my mom, she and I talked about how exciting it would be to create a talk show for tween girls.

The exciting thing about self-confidence is that it becomes the foundation for achieving any dream that you dare to dream. It's defined as a feeling of trust in one's abilities, qualities, and judgment. For me, the only thing that I knew was that I wanted to create a talk show. It never dawned on me that I couldn't do it. My parents supported all my dreams, and I believed in my dreams as well.

In the summer of 2013, I launched my very own YouTube talk show *Girls So Positive Motivational Minutes.* I started the first show with an introduction of the format to my future audience, and then I began asking many of my neighborhood friends and classmates to be guests on the new GSP talk show.

Each guest I asked agreed to come on the show. My mom set up our guest room as my TV studio with the lighting and cameras. It took much time to get it right finally, but afterward, we had fun making what seemed like an impossible dream come true. My guests appeared on the show to discuss topics relevant to tweens, such as choosing friends wisely, making the right decisions, sibling relationships, and much more. There was even a show all about my dad and me. I created over twelve segments and had over two thousand views on the show about choosing friends.

Having a dream is easy. But if you believe in your vision while creating a plan of action to make it happen, and be consistent in your approach to achieving your dreams, it will come true. Trust in yourself, surround yourself with people like your parents, close friends, and family members who believe in you. Ask for help. No rule in life says you must do it alone, plus, it's no fun working on your dream alone. It's exciting when you're building your vision around those who are in your corner cheering you on. It comes in handy when you hit the road bumps along the way. And trust me, there are many road bumps.

However, they are there to help you become stronger, wiser, and smarter. It's all in how you look at it.

As we continued producing shows for GSP, we became more creative with topics for the show. One show stands out to me the most. It was the taping of my brothers and me during our visit to Southern California. Whenever my brothers, Shang and Darius, and I are together, anything can happen. They are two of the most incredible brothers a sister can have. They always make me laugh. So many of my friends shared with me how they too were inspired to spend more quality time with their siblings after seeing our show.

As I look back on those days, which seemed so long ago, I'm so thankful that we were able to inspire others to be closer with their siblings. Isn't that what life is all about? Encouraging others to be a better version of themselves, finding the good in others, shining the light when others can only see darkness, and being your true authentic self. My mother once told me that being beautiful is to BEaUtiful.

After a year of taping, fifth grade was here. My classmates and I were beginning to see middle school in our vision, and we were feeling a bit nervous and excited at the same time. I attended Lowes Island Elementary School, where we had a fantastic after-school program. They offered so many classes for students to take. One of the classes that I chose was the Junior Toastmasters class. I learned the art of public speaking, which became a priceless gem for me, as I was able to develop my professional speaking skills. After graduating from the program, I became a certified Junior Toastmaster's Speaker.

Little did I know that what I learned in those classes would serve as the foundation for my confidence in public speaking.

My mom created a Girls So Positive curriculum and registered the program as an after-school enrichment class in 2014, the first-ever Girls So Positive after-school course and Girls So Positive News Show was launched at Lowes Island Elementary school for fifth-grade girls. The course taught the girls how to be comfortable speaking in front of an audience, present news in front of a camera, and the importance of self-confidence.

Once the class was announced, it filled up quickly. Two of my best friends, Lauryn and Lily Parks, were also a part of the class, and we couldn't wait for the first session to begin. I experienced a feeling of pride, as I knew that my mother would give the girls the golden nuggets that she had always given to me. I knew that the girls in our class would become confident and ready for middle school. And you know what? I was right.

I will never forget the first day. As we walked into the library, we each took a seat at the long table that my mom had set up for us and looked around with curious eyes as we couldn't help but notice the enormous yellow sheet of paper that covered the entire large table designated for our workspace. In the middle of the table were so many crayons and markers. Once we finished with the formalities of introductions, we were directed to find a space on the paper and begin writing a list of the good things that we liked about ourselves. We were then asked to present to our group each trait that stood out to us the most. Some of the girls' lists were long, and some were not.

A few weeks later, my mom asked us to repeat the same project, and as expected, each of our lists were longer and more complete than the first day of class. I can recall many parents speaking to my mom after each class as they picked up their daughters, and their comments all related to the level of confidence that each of their daughters had gained in themselves.

By the end of the course, each of us had produced our own show, which varied by interest. Some were on cooking, fashion, and style, just to name a few.

The Girls So Positive class went to another level when we created *GSP NEWS*, which consisted of each of us finding a topic that we were each passionate about, researching the issue, and reporting on our findings. This is by far one of my greatest memories. Today, the shows can be found on the So Positive YouTube channel. When I look back on those days, I often feel a sense of gratitude for my mom because she gave others the very tools that she gave to me.

It's one thing to be a young girl growing up in a world filled with so many choices and decisions to make, and it's another thing to grow up as a confident young girl in a world filled with so many options and decisions to make. There are two things that you can gain in life that no one can take away from you—knowledge and the power of self-confidence. Once you have it, you're empowered to change to the world.

I recently sat down with my mother to ask her why she felt so much compassion in helping so many girls within the Girls So Positive after-school program.

Here's an excerpt from our talk.

"For me, growing up was different than it is for you. My mother worked all the time, which meant that I didn't have much time to spend with her. There were so many things that I had to figure out by myself. I always knew that I wanted to raise robust, powerful, and confident daughters. I had a clear understanding of what it was going to take to achieve those goals. In addition to doing so, I felt the need to give back."

My mother was approached by many of the mothers of the GSP class, and their feedback was always positive. They would often tell my mother about the changes they'd noticed in their daughters and the amount of confidence that was exemplified, or in how their daughters had eye contact when they spoke to them.

I will always be proud of the gift that my mother and father gave me. And I will always be proud to be a Girl So Positive.

Creating Your Dreams

If you can dream it, you can do it.

– Walt Disney

Growing up, I struggled with my weight. To help me, my parents wanted to increase my physical activity and asked me if I was interested in participating in any fall or winter sports. Although I played tennis with my dad, I played mostly during the spring and summer.

I decided that I wanted to dance and cheer. When I was six, my mother registered me with the Reston Youth Association (RYA) in cheer. I had practices twice a week and a game every Saturday morning. My parents also enrolled me with the Reston Ballet. I was swamped and active. However, I soon lost interest in ballet and focused on cheer. It was a lot of fun, and it kept me engaged in physical activities for the year, but after the season was over, I was ready to move on.

At the age of seven, my pediatrician asked my mom to begin making my school lunches as a solution to control the foods that I was eating during the day.

Although my doctor never put me on a diet, she monitored my weight closely, as they were hoping it would even out as I grew.

During the spring and summer months, my father continued to coach me in tennis, and my grandfather instructed him to put me on the track so that I could begin practice running. I'm thankful for those moments because I was being prepared to be a part of Girls on the Run. I enjoyed playing tennis, but I did not enjoy running as much. Looking back, I see how I could have improved my game then by merely running after more balls.

When I was eight years old, our school invited a nutritionist to speak to us about the importance of making healthy food choices. After the nutritionist's visit, I felt as though my life had changed forever. I recall that day as being a day of enlightenment for me because I learned so much about food and how it affects your body. I decided that day to become a vegetarian. Noticed that I made the decision. Although I was only 8 years old, I knew that I wanted to feel better about my body. After I understood more about food and how to make better choices, I loved myself enough to make the right decision for me.

After school, I told my mother about the visit, and during dinner, I announced to my family that I would officially become a vegetarian. I told my parents that I wanted to eat healthy all the time. I decided to stop eating ice cream and cookies for dessert at school and at home. I began implementing all of the things that I learned at school during the nutritionist visit by reading food labels and serving size of everything before I would decide to eat it.

My family's reaction was extremely positive and supportive. They shared how proud they were of me for setting my goals, and they would support me all the way. I began to learn how to read food labels while gaining an understanding of what they meant.

In addition to my new decision, my parents continued to involve me in physical activities outside of school. They did so by registering me for Girls on the Run. My mom became one of the coaches, and thus I began running the track after school. I was so pleased with my progress. My dad and grandfather had prepared me for running.

No longer was it a chore but more of a choice that I had made for myself. I enjoyed running because it gave me a sense of accomplishment each time I would finish a lap around the track. Our group prepared for our first 5K run, a feat that I'd never attempted. But I was up for the challenge.

During training for my 5K, I would often ask my parents for a sports drink that was healthy and consisted of fewer sugars. I was feeling confident about my health and being from a family whose generations of elders had diabetes, I knew that I had to stop the cycle of unhealthy food choices that would often lead to diseases like the ones in my extended family.

Shopping around for sports drinks was a challenge. Everything seemed to have too much sugar. I knew what that meant, so I decided to go a different route. I would either continue to drink water, or I would mix my sports drink with additional water to dilute the sugar.

For the next five years, I became extremely disciplined with my food choices. My family would often watch with amazement as I turned down candy, cakes at parties, cookies at school, and ice cream at home. Once you experience the feeling of confidence in an area of your life that was not always present, you make sure to keep moving forward because nothing is better than feeling your best and looking your best. Yes, I felt terrific, and for the first time, I began to look amazing.

In June 2017, I was accepted into the Loudoun County Young Entrepreneurs Academy. I was there to create my first official company and launch my first product. This was an opportunity to put my vision for a healthy teen product in the marketplace. With the help of my mentor, Carole Stizza, and director K. C. Repage, along with the entire Loudoun County Chamber of Commerce, my dream was born. After a year of research, classes, presentations, feedback, trials and errors, my new product is now in its design stage to be the first, all-natural, healthy sports drink intended for teen athletes.

My new product is expected to replenish the vitamins and nutrients lost during physical activity, while also being a definite asset to the body by exclusively consisting of all-natural ingredients.

I've learned that the first step to achieving your goals is to have confidence in yourself. Believe in your abilities to achieve greatness, regardless of what it may look like on the outside. Knowing who you are on the inside will undoubtedly give you the foundation to stand firm. I've always been taught that nothing is impossible, because when someone tells you that your dream is impossible, kindly remind them by saying, "that *I'm possible*." **Did you notice that IMPOSSIBLE when separated is seen as I'M POSSIBLE.** That's powerful because you're possible, your dreams are possible, your vision is possible, your academic success is possible. Believe in your possibilities. Each night before I go to bed, I have a consistent routine that I never deviate from. One of the things I do is read my list of dream and visions that I have for myself and I tell myself that it's possible because I'M POSSIBLE. I encourage you to do the same because you're worth it. Look at yourself in the mirror and say "I'M POSSIBLE" because you are.

Today, I've been fortunate to have had several opportunities to speak in front of audiences as large as 500 people. My most memorable moment was accepting the invitation to give my first commencement speech at my alma mater at Lowes Island. Returning as a rising high school freshman humbled me because, at that moment, I realized that every step that we take in life is leading us to our most celebrated moments.

As a Silver Award Girls Scout, I understand the value of service and what it means to give back to our community. As a result, in August 2018, I've created the So Positive Initiative (SPI). SPI mentors 5th grade students to help them understand and develop their self-confidence as they matriculate into middle-school. The high school students that work with SPI have an opportunity to develop their leadership and public speaking skills along with earning volunteer and community service hours for their college application.

The memories of my fifth grade year served me all too well. I have full confidence in knowing that having a program like the SPI being offered to students can become their foundation for success and belief in their abilities to achieve greatness. My dream is to help each 5th grader gain the tools they need to help them to understand the value of what having self-confidence can do in their lives.

Points to ponder:

- There is never a dream too tall or too wide to achieve.

- Whatever your age, now is the perfect time to work toward your dream.

- Your dreams allow you to be in the driver's seat to your destiny.

- An idea means

I Dream Everyday About_____

(You can fill in the blank)

Be your own cheerleader. Don't allow others to tell you that your dreams are impossible. Just kindly remind them that *I'M POSSIBLE!*

Time for Tennis

My father gave me the greatest gift anyone could give another person. He believed in me.

– Jim Valvano

When I think about tennis, I think about my father, Shang Andrews. My mother often reminds me how fortunate I am to have a father who has given me all of who he is and more. I was four years old when he put a tennis racket in my small, yet opened and excited left hand. Yes, I'm a lefty.

Little did I know that he was planting the seeds of confidence, tenacity, consistency, mental toughness, and success in my hand. He would take my brother and me out to the tennis courts, and with a big bucket of balls, begin to test our hand-eye coordination by tossing the ball to each of us. I remember those days as being full of fun and laughter. My dad had a way of making everything fun for us. As I ponder on those days, he was creating an environment for us to enjoy while developing our mental and physical strength.

Tennis has become more than a game for me. It's my opportunity to develop into a great player and CEO. To become a great player, you must look at those who have achieved greatness in that area. For me, that champion is Serena Williams. I remember listening to an interview her dad gave about her ability to play the game. He predicted that she would one day become number one in the world. That prediction wasn't just because she was his daughter. He saw something great in Serena, and most importantly, he believed in her and what she could achieve. My dad is the same way. He says that he has always seen greatness in me and believes in me and in what I can achieve.

In 2007, Serena was interviewed on the *Charlie Rose* show and said, "My dad taught me winning is not important if it's done on the tennis court. He said, 'You're a winner if you're a winner in life.'" I can relate to that statement 100 percent. My dad has always taught me that tennis is first a mental game, and if I can achieve my mental game, I could accomplish any game. I have learned to understand that I don't need a trophy to confirm a win.

I was given my dad's secret recipe for success. He taught me to be confident enough in myself by doing the best that I can in the face of adversity and without quitting.

The amount of time that my dad has invested in me has played a large part in my success today. Imagine a 14-year-old continually being told *you're a champion, you're a winner.* For years, and even today, he consistently builds my mental game.

I remember when I first started playing tennis, 90% of my balls would go over the fence, and each time that I would lose a ball, my dad would say, "Wow, Alana, you're so strong. Great job!" For every positive word he spoke to me, I would begin speaking them to myself. I often find myself doing the same thing today. I continuously tell myself that I can do it, I'm never a quitter, and that I can do anything.

Tennis became my mental training ground. I've learned to believe in myself and in my ability to achieve greatness in anything. I refuse to quit on myself! There have been times when my schedule has been packed with school work, my company, and afterschool activities. It's so easy to say, "I'm tired." But that would only be an excuse, and excuses have never empowered anyone to greatness. I tell myself "Alana, this is what you 've dreamed of, this is what you want, and it will not come without a price." Whatever I need to tell myself to keep moving forward is my ultimate reward because, in the end, I've won by accomplishing my goal.

One of the phrases that I live by is "Make No Excuses....Have No Limitations." When you don't make excuses, you're setting yourself up to experience life to the fullest degree because you become limitless. When you make an excuse, you are limited to what you can do and where you can go. It's like putting yourself in an excuse box. For example, you may say "I can't do my homework because I have to visit a relative during the weekend." In that instant, you've limited yourself to not turning in your homework which means, you may have a not so favorable grade, and ultimately you may not be able to participate in a class discussion because the material that you were assigned to wasn't reviewed. Free yourself from excuses and live a limitless life.

There's no way that I could have ever achieved this belief on my own. I'm thankful for my father and his love and patience. But most of all, I'm grateful that he taught me the game of tennis, for it has become my most beloved sport.

Through tennis, I development mental toughness. It has prepared me to keep fighting. I understand now that there will be times when it will appear very challenging, and it may feel like I may be losing. But I tell myself just don't quit and to stay in the game. When I do so, I always come out a champion. And that's what matters the most.

Recently, I sat down with my dad for a talk, and I asked him to share with me the moment he knew that he had developed his self-confidence. This talk was significant to me because my dad is one of the greatest men that I know with an enormous amount of self-confidence. I see it in his walk, how he always holds his shoulder's back and his head up, how he speaks and the eye contact he always gives anyone that he may be speaking with. I'm always watching him because he's my teacher. I'm learning how to do so many things through my observation of him. I observe both my parents because they have traveled the road that I will have to one day travel on my own, and I want to be prepared. My biggest advice to my peers would be to honor your parents, learn from them and allow their words of wisdom to prepare you for your future.

I'm always inspired by my dad. Here's an excerpt from our talk: "I initially started playing tennis in California at the age of twelve in a summer program at Pepperdine University.

Tennis helped me fight my challenges in life, as it also helped to build my self-confidence. It's a sport that you must rely on your abilities to be successful. In the beginning, I had to understand if you are down 5 to 0, and the game is over at 6, you still have a chance to win. The challenge is coming back from almost impossible odds and then having the confidence to make it happen. This was the key for me. If I succeed, that meant that I have accomplished what almost seemed impossible, and I can build on that confidence. You have no one to point the finger to because you can only win by your own ability. It's you and you alone.

Once you accomplish a comeback from not winning any games that are literally at zero to winning the match, that experience instills a level of confidence that will carry you on throughout your life.

"In the classroom, no one could tell me what I couldn't achieve. If I am down, it is not over. If I must stay up all night, I will do whatever it takes to succeed, even if that means that I must ask my professor for extra time. Nothing is over until it's over."

My dad always told me that I could achieve anything if I put my mind to it. I believed him then, and I believe him now. What has worked for my dad, works for me. As I stated earlier in this chapter, tennis has taught me so many lessons that I've been able to apply in my everyday life.

My dad gave me some lessons that I would like to share with you. My goal is to help you during those times when you need to find the physical and mental strength in your game or at school to keep moving forward.

Lesson 1: Have Staying Power

Before you begin a sport, sign up for a class or even work toward your dream; it's important to understand what it will take to achieve success in that area. It's not advisable to go into anything with a blindfold, because you may just get blindsided. Study your field of interest and know what it will take to win. If it's a sport that you're in, there will be times when you must have the perseverance to keep going because you know that if you slow down, or even look back, it could cause you specific consequences, like a lost point or even the game. Tennis is an individual sport, and unless you're playing doubles, you have no choice but to depend on yourself. It's a game where you must understand that there's no set amount of time for each set. You could play for thirty minutes or an hour. Your mind-set must be on staying with it.

A great player will work out when no one is around and won't wait until practice when the coach is telling you to run so many laps around the track. Understand the game and know what it will take to win. Be mindful that success doesn't always come in winning the trophy, but in knowing that you did everything possible to be your best you in that sport. The mental prize is as good as a real award because you can rest that night knowing that you gave your 100 percent because of your staying power, and that's all any of us can give.

Lesson 2: Be Consistent

If there is one thing that will ensure your success in life, that is to learn how to be consistent. When my brother and I were very young, my dad would take us out to practice on the tennis courts, and he would have this big bucket of balls. He would work with my brother, and then he would work with me.

There were also times when he would work with both of us. We would do the same drills repeatedly. I didn't realize as much then as I do now, but my dad was consistently training us to develop quick hand-eye coordination. He was developing our muscle memory and our reflexes.

Today, my brother Shang and I can catch a ball without even thinking about it. Our reflexes have matured from over the many years of playing tennis together. What was once a challenge is now achievable. By dad consistently training us, we were able to sharpen our skills. Those skills have followed us in the classroom as well. For example, I have to consistently practice math to continue making good grades in the class. When you make an A on a test or a homework assignment, don't assume that you know everything. Math, in particular, builds from one level to the next. Therefore, you must be consistent in your studies to continue making the grade you're reaching for. Since I've developed the skills and understanding of what it means to be consistent, I know that by doing so, I am ensuring my success in school and in life.

Lesson 3: Be Mentally Tough

Being mentally tough in tennis has taught me to be mentally tough in my business, in school, during my speaking engagements, and life in general. When you are mentally prepared for a game, you tune everything out. The negative thoughts, the fear that tries to creep in, the nerves, the doubt. They're coming, but they don't have to stay. You're in control of what remains in your mind. My father taught me to be mentally tough by believing in myself and in what I can achieve on and off of the courts.

As Vince Lombardi said, "Mental toughness is many things and rather difficult to explain. Its qualities are sacrifice and self-denial. Also, most importantly, it is combined with a perfectly disciplined will that refuses to give in. It's a state of mind—you could call it a character in action."

Lesson 4: Quitting is Never an Option

There will be times when it's hard, and there's no sign of relief in your view. But be confident in knowing that the challenge is making you better mentally and physically. Trust me, comfort comes, and when it does, you'll enjoy the victory much more because you didn't quit. These same principles apply to our everyday lives. My dad has told me many stories about his experience in college. He once said to me that there were times when he couldn't figure out a math problem. He would stay up all night working on it, and he would eventually solve the equation. He said that his experience in tennis helped him get through college because he never quit on the court, and he would never quit on math. It was just never an option.

Lesson 5: Have Fun!

The one thing that I loved about being a kid was that we spent so much of our time playing with our friends in our neighborhood. When you enter middle school and even high school, things change because you have more schoolwork to focus on. My parents have always taught me to balance my life by living our family mantra. *We work hard, and we play hard.* When it's time to work, all my focus is on my studies, and I have done well because I give it 100 percent. But, when it's time to play, I play.

Whether I'm on vacation with my family or just talking to my friends. I make sure that I enjoy the moment and have the best time that I can have. I give it 100 percent because it keeps me balanced and happy.

The Art of Friendship

L ots of people want to ride with you in the limo, but what you want is someone who will take the bus with you when the limo breaks down.

– Oprah Winfrey

When I think about the art of friendship, I think about everything that goes into creating something that has the potential to blossom into beauty from any view. Art itself is seen from many perspectives, yet it's fulfilling for all that has an appreciation and value for it's presence. For example, when creating new friendships and maintaining the ones you've had for many years, you must think about all the ingredients that go into creating something beneficial for everyone to appreciate.

A key point to remember is something my mother taught me a long time ago. She said to always be willing to give more than you receive. There's so much truth to those words. You give because that's something you want to do, and you don't leave with an expectation that others should do the same. You position yourself to experience more of the joy behind giving than the disappointment of not receiving.

When creating the art of friendship, you must have and be willing to use the proper tools to make it work. First, you'll need good listening skills. My mother has always reminded me that we have two ears and one mouth. To me, that means that we should listen more and talk less. When you use your ability to listen attentively to others, there are so many opportunities to learn about them and what they have to say. People become interested in you when you show an equal amount of interest in them.

Another tool to use in creating the art of friendship is being able to resolve problems by effectively communicating your thoughts without offending others. Everyone has feelings, and it's important that we remain mindful of how our words can be powerful enough to make someone feel really great about themselves, yet at the same time, our words can do the opposite and make someone feel very bad as well.

When I was nine years old, my mom taught me one of the greatest lessons on the power behind decisions and consequences. I learned that decisions and consequences are inseparable twins, wherever decisions go, consequences are always beside her. A key point to remember is that BEFORE you make a decision, always, think about the consequece that is standing right next to it. That is one lesson that I have always kept very close to me. When I am speaking with my friends, I'm constantly thinking about my choice of words because I don't want to offend or hurt their feelings. And if I do, I make sure that I am quick to offer a sincere apology. I understand that the consequence of anything that I decide to say or do is right there and a I've learned how to take the time to think about whether or not I am ok with the consequence that will follow any of my decisions.

When you are in the beginning phase of creating new friendships, there will be some that will last for a short while, and there will be some that will last a lifetime. The beauty of it all is that you are constantly learning things about yourself. You'll grow, and you may decide that although last year you enjoyed spending time with a friend because you shared a common interest, you may also realize that you have other interests which may bring more friends. The friends that will last are the ones that aren't based on conditions. A true friend will stay with you regardless of your new found interests, they aren't controlling and are totally understanding when you may want to enjoy a new activity with another person.

During the developmental stages of creating friendships, you'll find yourself learning more about yourself and growing into a more sensitive and caring person. You'll continue to develop characteristics of being kind, thoughtful, trustworthy, supportive, and caring. When you find yourself developing into this type of person, one that will protect those that they genuinely care for and love, the thought of hurting that individual is off the shelf.

So, why does it seem like finding that one good friend can sometimes be so hard? Well, at 14 years old, I've developed some theories on why the challenge can be a great feat. Today, many teens are becoming less social because it has become more comfortable for them to hide behind a screen. They tend to build up a false image of themselves to create "social friends," when in reality, a true friend is not one that you have to justify by the numbers of "likes" that they have given you as a stamp of approval.

Our generation, which is formally called Generation Z (those born between 1996 and 2010), is sometimes pressured into being perfect. Some feel the need to always look flawless. Is a flaw something that's different?

How does being different equate to being something that's negative? There isn't a person who has ever been born as perfect and flawless. Once we embrace ourselves with true acceptance of who we are is when we can do the same for others. This is when the journey of finding a true friend can begin.

When my mom and I wrote the lyrics to my song It Doesn't Matter, we focused on topics that dealt with self-love, bullying, self- acceptance and just being okay with who you are. I was still developing my self-confidence and self-esteem. This allowed me to be open to finding a true friend. That was never my main priority. I believed in letting things happen when they're meant to happen, and lucky enough, it did.

I was in the first grade when I met a set of triplets who would not only become my best friends for life, but they each became my sisters. Laury, Lily and Layne Parks are the most amazing people you'll ever meet. They have three distinct personalities, and they each have the most amazing and colorful dreams. They're also extremely talented musicians. I admire them so much. We are able to bring out the best in each other, and I have so much love and admiration for them.

It's always important to surround yourself with people who support you, so when you accomplish something, they will be by your side to cheer you on. I have found that when you're in an environment where others' main goal is to tear you down, there's no room to flourish and explore your real abilities. The art of friendship is the art of love, support, honesty, trustworthiness, equality, and happiness. That is something that Lauryn, Lily, Layne and I each share.

Within the art of friendship are certain components that make it complete. Below is a list of those components:

The Art of Love

Love can have various meanings, and all definitions are a matter of how you see it. I see love as the act of not giving up on someone when there is a conflict. I see love as being very rare, as it mostly occurs when someone is their true self around others. The triplets and I have been friends for my eight years. They are not just my friends but have become my sisters. Through any obstacle we may face, love is there to overcome it.

The Art of Support

Support is defined as letting a friend know that one is behind them in whatever they do and that one will support them in the decision they make is a good foundation for friendship. The triplets and I have supported each other during those days of the elementary school variety shows when we were on stage dressed in our costumes and danced to our favorite song to supporting each other during band camp in middle school and more. No matter what we're doing or where we are, we can count on each other for unconditional support.

The Art of Honesty

It is essential not to hide something from another when you think it's in their best interest. Although the truth may hurt, it's always what we need to hear, as it may affect our future encounters. Honesty can be the reason why you trust someone, or the reason why you don't, which goes along with the art of trustworthiness.

The Art of Trust

The act of trust can take a while until it is given to another. We may only trust ourselves because we may not be completely comfortable in trusting someone else. The more time you spend with a friend, you're given opportintues to see examples of their character which will inadvertently begin to allow you to build your trust in them. It's not always about what someone says, it's what they do that gives you a true reflection of who they are. You'll know when you begin to feel comfortable enough to trust them. Don't rush into it. Remember, progress is a process that takes time.

The Art of Equality

I see balance as the action of both partners having a fair say. This ensures that not one person would be soaring over the other, but both will come to a fair ground and decide what's best for the all involved.

The Art of Happiness

It is essential that friendships are filled with happiness and positive energy. This creates the space for you to be free in the being your most beautiful you. This gives you the freedom to be open to trying new things together. Happiness will allow you to entirely be ready to give your best self to someone in a friendship.

True friendship will last through many challenges. It's solid and unbreakable. When I was younger, I often thought that having hundreds of friends would be the best experience ever. But as I've matured over the years, I appreciate the quality of my friendships rather than the quantity.

I'm fortunate to have found Lauryn, Lily, and Layne who will be there for me no matter what. And I will be there for them as well. They have always supported me with kindness and honesty. The art of friendship is beauty from any perspective.

Being Different Makes the Difference

You are the only person on earth that can use your ability.

– Zig Ziglar

"People may often say that this or that person has not yet found himself. But the self is not something that one finds. It is something one creates." according to Thomas Szasz, noted psychiatrist. This statement represents the acceptance of having to create yourself and knowing that great things take time.

Our middle school years are a time of transformation and self-discovery. We often find ourselves questioning who we are. That's normal, and it's okay. I asked myself the same question, and I distinctively remember telling myself that I am just like them. For some reason, I felt that being like them was the ideal situation. I thought it was what made me stand out, but it's what made me blend in.

Throughout the years, I've continued to notice the unique qualities about myself that makes up the essence of who I am. I've learned to value and appreciate every aspect of me which is how I've grown to absolute love myself.

As I continue to grow and develop, the lessons of my parents seem to be clearer. The lesson of decisions and consequences have really come in handy during those middle school years. I understand clearly how they're always connected, whether for good or bad reasons. The decision that you make can sometimes have the most substantial effect in the smallest situations. One careless decision can create a significant consequence. Throughout life, you will be tested to choose what's best and right for yourself. I have consistently found myself going into more profound thought about the consequence of every action I decide to make. I ask myself, "What's the best and worst outcome from this, and do I want to accept the worst?"

Often, we may be so caught up in the moment that we forget to think about this fundamental question. I have witnessed many people who simply chose not to pay attention to this question. We may often make excuses for why we don't think things through. For example, we may say, "It's only this one time," or, "Everyone else is doing it, so it can't be that bad." Over time these excuses will add up and create a negative environment, which could've been prevented if the consequences from the decisions had been considered.

"Excuses are tools of incompetence used to build monuments of nothingness." - Unknown. My father taught me this quote, and I have made it a point to live by those words. My mother often tells me that she's proud of me because she's never encountered a time when I've given her excuses for anything. I'm so thankful that she sees this in me, and I am also appreciative of my father who imparted those words of wisdom for me to live by. If there is a goal to reach, an assignment that must be done, a promise that you made to a friend or a chore that you are assigned to, don't make an excuse for why it can't be done. Just do it.

The feeling of accomplishing your goal to complete any task is larger than the work itself. It's priceless because it aids in your growth and development and more importantly, it builds your self-confidence because when you consistently accomplish any goal that you've set out to do, your belief in yourself becomes insurmountable. Refusing to make excuses has become part of who I am.

Every day we're given an opportunity to grow into being more than who we were the day before. The choice to accept these opportunities can generally stand between a thin line of excuses. For example, the thought of fear may creep into our heads when an opportunity is given to us regarding public speaking. We can choose to accept the challenge or make an excuse and not give ourselves a chance to even try.

Explanations are a way to convince ourselves the truth of a false reality. I have learned that they only lead us to miss out on events in life. Therefore, it is extremely wise to limit the use of them as much as possible.

Being different means knowing yourself and understand what drives you to accomplish certain goals. One of the things that drive me is my competitiveness. I have found that in any activity, task, or game, I've always had a desire to succeed. My dad and are very similar when it comes to competing. When we're on the tennis court, I'm ready for the challenge. When my brother and I are going to the car, although he may casually walk to take his seat, I'm always trying to challenge him to the front seat.

At a young age, I was taught the lesson of hard work. I was told that if you work hard enough at anything, the results will be in your favor. I've applied these lessons to the activities I participated in, as I expected positive results. Every time there was an obstacle, I put on my "game face" and figured out a way to get the odds back on my side. As I continued to have this mind-set, others soon became uncomfortable with me. I began to feel that my competitiveness was not something that everyone approved of.

When you're in middle school it's challenging enough as you're learning more about yourself, taking a rigorous course load and involved in extracurricular activities. So, when your peer group shows signs of disapproval towards your drive to be competitive, it can be a challenge. But, what helped me through those challenges was one of my most beloved quotes. I referenced it at the beginning of the first chapter, "Because one believes in oneself, one doesn't try to convince others. Because one is content with oneself, one doesn't need others' approval. Because one accepts oneself, the whole world accepts him or her." – Lao Tzu.

When you decide to accept yourself and your differences, some may choose to join you and others may not. Know that it's okay and wish the best for everyone. My mom has always told me that we're each on our path of self-discovery. I'm so grateful for my parent's wisdom and knowledge. It has help me so much as I grow and development into a young lady.

During my eighth-grade school year, I had decided to run for student body president. I knew that this opportunity would benefit me, as I would have to use my leadership skills on a regular basis. Once I had a vision of myself being in the position, I knew that I wouldn't be able to give it up. A few days later I recorded my video and presented my points on how I would make a great president.

During this time, false rumors had been going around on how I'd been passing out candy and pins for the election, which was not allowed. At that time, I had to make a decision and think about the consequences of how to handle things. I could either waste energy being upset, or I could use my competitive nature to use a unique strategy. I soon learned that you can't please everyone because of the difference in opinions we all have. I started focusing on what I could control with my competitive mind-set still in play.

I was honored to be elected student body president and was reminded that whatever I put my mind to do, I could achieve. I now know that each of our differences allows us to share a unique story that can hopefully help another person. What many people may call competitive, I call my desire to succeed, as it allowed me to focus on what I could accomplish.

My final point to share in how being different makes the difference is in how I like to always be two steps ahead of the game. I'm a planner and a forward thinker. Some of my peers often comment on how they're just focused on what's for lunch or what's for dinner. For me, I'm in the next two days or so. Whatever works best for how you like to operate is what you should go with. Being in tune with yourself and understanding how you perform wil not only make you different but it will also help you to succeed. the

Although this is true, it's essential to have a plan to accomplish your goals. I often think about my plans and the path I should take to get there. Some of my peers have said, "you're too mature." The way they've said it was meant to be an insult, but I chose to see it as a compliment. Others added that I work "too hard." I've never really seen the negative meaning behind this statement just because it is implying that I focus on working toward what I would like to achieve. The thought process of wanting to plan for the future is nothing to be ashamed of, but rather proud of wanting to know your path.

Throughout life, there will be experiences that help create who you will become. No one finds themselves and is done creating who they are, because that indicates that you are finished learning. Every lesson builds a story. Every place makes a memory. Every person originates a relationship. Each person's experience in life is far from identical, so why do we feel the need to fit in? There is no point in covering up our original qualities when they were given to us for the purpose to help others.

We can learn so much from uncovering someone else's story, but if we all try to have the same one, then what is there to discover? I haven't finished finding the traits that make me who I am, but I have seen some. Each attribute delivers a message. What's yours?

Embrace Who You Are

*N*oble and great. Courageous and determined. Faithful and fearless. That is who you are and who you have always been. And understanding it can change your life because this knowledge carries a confidence that cannot be duplicated any other way.

– Sheri L. Dew

When someone is rejected, he or she may feel that they are not being accepted for who they are. In middle school, I wanted to be well known and to stand out. I didn't quite understand why I felt that way; I just knew that I wanted to be the one to make the final decision.

I always felt extremely comfortable speaking in front of the classroom or taking the lead and delegating roles in group projects. For someone in middle school, this can be a little odd because you begin to see that there aren't many of your peers doing the same things, or even interested in talking about their plans for the next five or even ten years from now. At times, I felt that I had to downplay my interests just to make others more comfortable when they were around me.

I've discovered my strengths and places where I need to focus my attention. As soon as I realized who I'm living for—which is me—I started spending more time thinking about myself and my future. This opened up an entirely new world for me as I learned more about who I was and what I wanted to do.

I found that my calling was in entrepreneurship, and within that, I needed to continue to build my leadership skills. I soon realized that in order to become a business leader I had to become a student of leadership. My parents enrolled me into the Loudoun County Young Entrepreneur's Academy (YEA). I also realized that I had to utilize my knowledge of confidence to know and believe who I am and who I will become. I thought that a bright place to practice those skills was at my school.

Leadership has always been a trait that I have loved and being a leader will still be a role I will fulfill. To bring that sense of confidence of a leader to my school, I gave the impression to my classmates that I was "full of myself" and a "try hard." I became aware of the negative comments I was receiving. I was puzzled how the comment of me being a "try hard" became negative, but really, I took it as a compliment. I believe that a leader, or a person in general, should always feel the need to "try hard" to reach success, so by them calling me a "try hard," it was a way of calling me successful. Another comment that came to my attention was be being "full of myself."

After hearing this comment, I didn't quite understood what it meant, but I soon figured it out. To be "full of yourself" is to love yourself constantly, to love yourself constantly is to have confidence within yourself, and to have confidence within yourself creates a leader. So yes, I am "full of myself," because I am a leader. Although some comments did confuse me, most of them inspired and motivated me to continue to follow my path. This experience was one of many that created skills that I would use later.

The comments that I heard from my classmates didn't stop me, because the same year, I was voted student body president. Yes, this may be odd hearing because the people who voted for me were the people who doubted me, but it does come to show that if you keep pursuing your dreams, goals, and improving yourself, others will grow to respect you and believe in you as well. Being student body president created so many new opportunities for me and pushed me to be a leader. I would stay up late at night and get up early in the morning to plan for the lessons and to build new ideas for the events we were expecting in student government. I made PowerPoint presentations for the meetings and had a structured plan so we could accomplish what we needed to get done.

During the sessions, I always remembered to listen to everyone's opinions and ideas and consider them. Although I was respectful, responsible, and kind, the negative comments continued, but it was the confidence that was built into me that carried me on. It was clear that no matter what I did, hatred and negativity would follow. I learned to laugh it off and to look at the positive side to everything. I knew I was still demonstrating the qualities of a leader, which was all I cared about because I was becoming one step closer to fulfilling my dream. I embraced who I was and never felt the need to hide.

Hiding is a sign of fear of rejection, and rejections only create new opportunities, therefore embracing my true self was setting me up for excellent opportunities.

To embrace yourself means to accept your uniqueness. I have listed some ideas on how you can begin the process of embracing yourself. This will help you to build your self-confidence because you will be starting at a place of self-respect, self-acceptance, and self-love. The magic about this exercise is that once you begin to accept yourself and love yourself with respect, you're able to freely do the same for others.

Remember...

Everything first begins with yoU because yoU are Unique, and yoU are enoUgh.

- First thing in the morning after you awake, tell yourself that you are amazing and today will be your best day ever!

- When you first look in the mirror, say hello to yourself and compliment something about yourself. For example. Good morning, _____. You are so beautiful, and I love your beautiful smile in the morning. It's the first thing that I notice about you, and it makes me happy to see you like this.

- Take a moment to find something about your hair that you like. Try a new style, or if you like the style, you already have, like it even more.

- Wiggle your toes with excitement and stretch your feet. Be kind to them.

- Breathe in good thoughts and exhale the negative ones. Breathing is known to make you healthier by reducing stress. So, keep breathing. 😊

- Open your eyes and stare at yourself in the mirror. Speak to your beautiful self. Give yourself a compliment and make plans for today. You'll be surprised by what a plan can do for your day. It will keep your mind focused and directed on your goals.

- Play some inspiring music. If there are others in your home who may be asleep, be sure to keep the volume low, or wear earbuds. This is your special moment to make it all about yoU.

- If there is something that you have to address at school, such as a homework assignment, a test, quiz, presentation, et cetera, make sure that you plan your days to prepare in advance for the assignment.

- You'll be surprised at the amount of confidence you will have when you're prepared for school. It makes such an amazing difference in how you feel and even in how you see yourself. You'll automatically see yourself as happy and as someone who's in control. Your walk will be different because confidence gives you a certain walk that is filled with security. It's a walk that makes you feel so very proud of yourself and your accomplishments.

- Therefore, preparation is the ultimate way to keep you building your self-confidence in school. Don't procrastinate. Just do it.

- Be mindful of your thoughts. If you notice something about you that you normally complain about, turn the complaint around to a compliment. There are so many things to be thankful for when it comes to ourselves.

- Lastly, be the best you that you can be today. Take it one day at a time since that's all that we have for the day. Enjoy it, embrace it, and embrace who yoU are.

Words from the
Wisdom of Others

I have not failed. I've just found 10,000 ways that won't work.

– *Thomas A. Edison*

My parents have always encouraged me to dream my biggest dream, and they've cheered me on every step of the way. Not once have they ever told me that there's something that I can't do, or that my idea wasn't good enough.

I've tried so many things, from creating new recipes that my brother Darius would said needed more work to creating a nine-hole golf course inside our home (made out of construction paper, of course☺). I've had many failures, but failure is the only path available to creating dreams out of unlimited possibilities.

Remember earlier when I told you about my first music CD? I was seven, and my family didn't have any experience in writing, producing music, or making videos. But we all got together to try, and we succeeded. There were a lot of failures along the way, but each failure taught us how to do it better. It was the only way we learned what did and did not work.

Embrace failure because it's a learning tool for greatness. It helps you move another step toward your dream. And most importantly, it builds your confidence because you'll begin to depend on it as a guide, a teacher, and a motivator to keep moving forward.

To help inspire you, I've compiled some quotes by people who have turned failure into success:

1. "Failure isn't fatal, but failure to change might be."
   – John Wooden

2. "Everything you want is on the other side of fear."
   - Jack Canfield

3. "Success is most often achieved by those who don't know that failure is inevitable."
   – Coco Chanel

4. "Only those who dare to fail greatly can ever achieve greatly." *– Robert F. Kennedy*

5. "The phoenix must burn to emerge." *– Janet Fitch*

6. "If you're not prepared to be wrong, you'll never come up with anything original." *– Ken Robinson*

7. "Giving up is the only sure way to fail."
   – Gena Showalter

8. "If you don't try at anything, you can't fail...it takes backbone to lead the life you want."
   – Richard Yates

9. "Failure should be our teacher, not our undertaker. Failure is delay, not defeat. It is a temporary detour, not a dead end. Failure is something we can avoid only by saying nothing, doing nothing, and being nothing."
   – Denis Waitley

10. "When you take risks, you learn that there will be times when you succeed and there will be times when you fail, and both are equally important."
    – Ellen DeGeneres

11. "When you start seeing your worth, you'll find it harder to stay around people who don't."
    –Unknown

12. "There is no failure except in no longer trying."
    – Chris Bradford

13. "Always remember you are braver than you believe, stronger than you seem, and smarter than you think *– Christopher Robin*

14. "Success is not final, failure is not fatal: it is the courage to continue that counts."
    – Winston Churchill

15. "There is only one thing that makes a dream impossible to achieve: the fear of failure."
    – Paulo Coelho

16. "Pain is temporary. Quitting lasts forever."
    – Lance Armstrong

17. "Success is stumbling from failure to failure with no loss of enthusiasm." *– Winston Churchill*

18. "I'd rather be partly great than entirely useless."
    – Neal Shusterman

19. "I've missed more than 9000 shots in my career. I've lost almost 300 games. Twenty-six times I've been trusted to take the game winning shot and missed. I've failed over and over and over again in my life. And that is why I succeed."
    - Michael Jordan

20. "The only real mistake is the one from which we learn nothing." *– Henry Ford*

21. "Failures are finger posts on the road to achievement." *– C. S. Lewis*

22. "Winners are not afraid of losing. But losers are. Failure is part of the process of success. People who avoid failure also avoid success."
    – Robert T. Kiyosaki

23. "Every adversity, every failure, every heartache carries with it the seed of an equal or greater benefit." **– Napoleon Hill**

24. "You build on failure. You use it as a stepping-stone. Close the door on the past. You don't try to forget the mistakes, but you don't dwell on it. You don't let it have any of your energy, or any of your time, or any of your space." **– Johnny Cash**

25. "It's not how far you fall, but how high you bounce that counts." **– Zig Ziglar**

26. "Failure is so important. We speak about success all the time. It is the ability to resist failure or use failure that often leads to greater success. I've met people who don't want to try for fear of failing."
    - J. K. Rowling

27. "Don't be afraid to fail. Don't waste energy trying to cover up failure. Learn from your failures and go on to the next challenge. It's ok to fail. If you're not failing, you're not growing." - *H. Stanley Judd*

28. "When we give ourselves permission to fail, we, at the same time, give ourselves permission to excel." – *Eloise Ristad*

29. "With a hint of good judgment, to fear nothing, not failure or suffering or even death, indicates that you value life the most. You live to the extreme; you push limits; you spend your time building legacies. Those do not die." – *Criss Jami*

30. "What is the point of being alive if you don't at least try to do something remarkable?"
    – *John Green*

ACKNOWLEDGMENTS

This book would have not been written without the support of those that have been with me and believed in me.

I am grateful for those that I've had the pleasure of working with as I've grown and developed into the young business leader that I am today.

The many examples that have been set before me and the words of encouragement that have echoed in my ears are the stepping stones that I've had the opportunity to walk on as I consistently move towards my dreams.

Someone who inspires you, is someone who has had a large positive impact on you. I am extremely fortunate to have such phenomenal parents who continue to love and support me every second of the day. Ever since a young age, my mother and father have set an example of what it means they carry the essential traits of respect, responsibility, kindness, trustworthiness, positivity, confidence, wisdom, and a determined attitude. I now have learned that each of these qualities has help me throughout every day and counters, as they also teach me more about myself.

My parents are the strongest, smartest, and kindest people I have ever known. They never settle to be average, but instead they reach greatness. I am so thankful to have such incredible parents who never cease to amaze me. So, when I am asked who is my biggest inspiration? There is no doubt in my mind that my parents aren't just on the list, but they define the list. Thank you, mom and dad, for always being by my side, supporting me, and inspiring me, and for that, I have confidence to continue my journey.

To my grandfather, Jimmie Lee Andrews, I love you for being wise and for always being a great father to my dad. I am the product of your inspiration and guidance within my father's life. Everything that you've given to him, he has given to me. Thank you for the gift of confidence.

To my most beloved grandmothers, Uncle Don and Aunt Ellie. I value your words of wisdom, and I am thankful that you've left me the blueprints to the many paths that I may take in life.

To Shang and Darius, you have always found a way to make me laugh and keep me grounded. You're continually supporting me in everything that I do. You're indeed the best brothers every. Amy and Desmond, thank you for being beautiful sisters. I admire you for the accomplishments that you've achieved in your life, and I appreciate you for setting the example of what a sister should be.

To Mr. Shaffer, thank you for being a supportive middle school principal, and Ms. Robinson, you've been the most significant guidance counselor and role model for any student that have met you. I'm grateful for the entire administrative and teaching staff at River Bend Middle School. You'll always have a place dear to my heart.

K.C. Repage, Program Director of the Young Entrepreneur's Academy and Tony Howard, President & CEO of Loudoun County Chamber of Commerce. Thank you so much for giving me the tools to become a young business leader, and I'm especially grateful for the many opportunities that I've had during as a student and now an alumnus of the program. Your consistent support of my projects will never go unnoticed.

To my mentor Carole Stizza, thank you for writing the forward to my book and for spending an entire year with me. I'll never forget how you came to support me during my first trade show and the other times you've supported me during the many meetings as I worked to develop my first product. I look forward to when its' released in the market.

To Mrs. Tina R. Johnson, thank you for the opportunity to speak at the 10th Annual 2018 Virginia's Women's Conference. I'll never forget when you spoke to me about the importance of paying it forward. Your example of leadership has given me the blueprint for how I will also conduct my business by paying it forward to help others.

To Mr. Marty Shoup from Blue Lion Multimedia. Thank you for taking the time to support YEA and for my first photo shoot. Your passion to help the students of the Young Entrepreneur's Academy will always mean so much to me.

To Mrs. Haidari and Mr. Cottone, your enthusiasm for this book has been inspiring. I will always appreciate the amount of support you've given me from the first day we've met, and you've always given sound advice and words of wisdom at the right time. Thank you.

Dr. Wolfe, thank you for believing in me and allowing me the opportunity to follow through with my dreams at Potomac Falls High School. I remember our first meeting as I sat in your office to ask for approval of the SPI program. Thank you for seeing the potential in the organization. I'm certain that the years ahead at PFHS will be filled with lots of growth and fun memories as I prepare for college.

To Michelle Parks and Heather Mason. For the past seven years, I have had so many opportunities to experience the power of community service within the Girls Scouts organizations. You two have been true examples of leadership. Because of the time that you've consistently invested in me and our troop, I've grown to understand the value of community service and the power of giving back. I know that I have a responsibility to help others and because of your leadership, I am prepared to serve our community through programs such as the So Positive Initiative. Thank you for your many sacrifices over the years.

To my best friends and my sisters, Lauryn, Lily and Layne Parks. We have been friends since the first grade, and I hope that the chapter on the Art of Friendship will allow readers to understand the powerful of friendship that has bonded us as sisters for life. Thank you for being my best friends and for your unconditional love for me and for each other.

APPENDIX A:
SUGGESTED MOTIVATIONAL SONGS

I've compiled a list from the collection of motivational and inspirational songs that my mom began playing for me as a child. As I've grown older, I've begun to add to the list to make it my own. Try waking up each morning with a song to inspire you so that you'll begin to feel amazing inside and out. These songs will inspire you to feel great about yourself and most importantly, build the bridge to creating your confidence.

Feel free to add to the list and share it with me on my Instagram page. I would love to hear from you.

1. "It Doesn't Matter" – Alana Andrews
2. "Beautiful Flower" – India Arie

3. "Roar" – Katy Perry

4. "Stronger" – Kelly Clarkson

5. "Rise Up" – Andra Day

6. "Best Day of My Life" – American Authors

7. "Have it All" – Jason Mraz

8. "Scars to your Beautiful" – Alessia Cara

9. "Symphony" – Clean Bandit featuring Zara Larsson

10. "On Top of the World" – Imagine Dragons

11. "High Hopes" – Panic at the Disco

12. "Invincible" – Kelly Clarkson

13. "Reflection" - Christina Aguilera

14. "I Am Not My Hair" – India Arie

15. "Break the Shell" – India Arie

16. "Who Says" – Selena Gomez

17. "India.Aire" – India Arie

18. "Lovely Day" - Bill Withers

19. "Happy" – Pharrell Williams

20. "Hero" – Moriah Carey

ABOUT THE AUTHOR

Alana Andrews is Generation Z's newest business leader who has the insight and knowledge of understanding what the power of self-confidence can do in a person's life. She's the 14 years old, Author, Speaker, Founder & CEO of So Positive, LLC based in Potomac Falls, VA. So Positive is innovative in its approach by creating products that are designed to help today's youth build their self-confidence while also maintaining a healthy lifestyle.

In the spring of 2018, Alana graduated from the Loudoun County Young Entrepreneur's Academy where she worked with mentors and business leaders. There she developed a soon to be released new and innovative product designed for teen athletes. It will be the first of its kind.

As a Silver Award Girls Scout, Alana understands the value of service and what it means to give back to her community. As a result, she's founded the So Positive Initiative which is an acronym for (SPI). SPI mentors 5th grade students to help them understand and develop their self-confidence as they matriculate into middle-school. The high school students that work with SPI have an opportunity to develop their leadership and public speaking skills along with earning volunteer and community service hours for their college applications.

In 2017, Alana self-published her first book entitled Timeless, which is a book of inspirational poetry written for all ages. Alana's passion has also been to help others develop their self-confidence. As a student, she sees first-hand how the lack of self-esteem can affect a student's grades, body image of themselves and social interactions.

As a result, she was inspired to publish her second book Creating Confidence. Creating Confidence gives you an in-depth blueprint on how you can overcome obstacles, project self-assurance and rise to your highest potential.

Alana shares everything on the subject with readers, from sound advice, personal stories, self-tested techniques to try out, as well as over a dozen or so inspirational quotes from some of today's foremost celebrities.

At 14-years-old, Alana has spent half her life working towards her dream as the CEO of her own company. In 2011, she co-wrote and produced her first music CD entitled "It Doesn't Matter" to address the issues of bullying among elementary students.

In 2012, Alana created a Girls So Positive YouTube channel and worked with her mom to produce a talk show called Girls So Positive Motivational Minutes. Guests appeared on the show to discuss topics relevant to tweens such as bullying, making the right decisions, sibling relationships, the art of cooking and more.

In 2014, the first-ever Girls So Positive afterschool program formally called the Girls So Positive News, launched at Lowes Island Elementary school for 5th-grade girls. The club taught by Alana's mom focused on teaching girls how to be comfortable speaking in front of an audience, present news materials in front of a camera, and the importance of self-confidence and self-love.

Alana is respected within the Loudoun County community by graduating from prestigious programs, earning top awards and recognition in the following areas:

- 2018 Harvard University Young Women's Business Leaders Conference

- 2018 Graduate of the Young Entrepreneurs Academy

- Recipient of the 2018 Sterling Ruritan Community Award

- Recipient of the 2018 Girls Scout Silver Award

- Recipient of the 2018 National Junior Honor Society

- Recipient of the 2018 NJHS Outstanding Achievement Award and Scholarship Winner

- Recipient of the 2018 Student Body President's Award

- Commencement Speaker at Lowes Island Elementary School 2018 Graduation Ceremony

- Recipient of the 2017 Ben Lacey Leadership Award

- Recipient of the 2017 Thomas Jefferson High School Leadership Conference Certificate

Alana plans to attend Standford University in the fall of 2022 where she will major in International Business. She's also an active member of DECA at her high school.

When Alana is not studying or running her company, she's on the tennis court with her Dad and brother, Shang. She's a professionally trained tennis player and has been playing since the age of 4-years-old. She is planning on playing for the Potomac Falls High School Tennis Team in the spring of 2019. In addition to tennis, Alana also enjoys playing, volleyball, watching movies with her brother, Darius, playing with her dog Keba, making music, and cooking with her mom.

My Journey through Pictures

Be yourself; everyone else is already taken.

— *Oscar Wilde*

I'm thankful to have had a community of support throughout my life. I wanted to share my journey in pictures of those that have been a part of my path to building self-confidence.

My parents are the absolute love of my life. I would not be where I am today without their love for me and their consistent belief and confidence in who I am and what I can do.

This was my first investor panel competition in 2018 through the Young Entrepreneur's Academy (YEA) which was one of the most life-changing opportunities I've ever experienced.

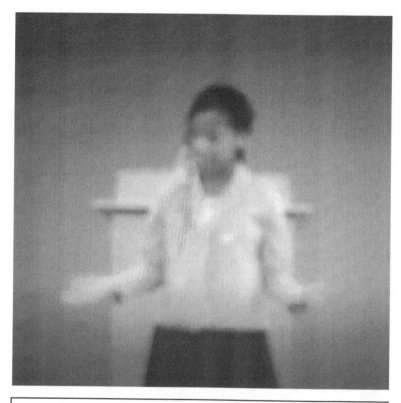

I was 11 years old when I was invited to my first speaking event in Washington, DC.

Mr. Fritz, Assistant Principal at River Bend Middle School is another example of having your school as a community of support. When teens feel safe, secure and supported, they can focus on being their best self. River Bend provided that support for me every day during school

The Program Director of the Young Entrepreneur's Academy, K.C. Repage has been a major part in helping me to develop my company and create a product from concept to formation. I've gained an insurmountable amount of experience and knowledge from this highly recommended program.

My middle school counselor Ms. Robinson always made herself available to me during school. Each day she would always give me the biggest smile and a warm hello. I remember having a speaking engagement one day, and she was there in the audience to support me. I will always be thankful for her presence in my life. In this picture we were at the 8th grade end-of-year awards ceremony.

I've been a girl scout since the age of 7, and my Girls Scouts Troop Leaders Mrs. Heather Mason and Mrs. Michelle Parks have always been so dedicated and loyal in their support of our troop. From driving us to programs to hosting meetings at their home, they've been there. They are true examples of being passionate about something that you believe in. We are pictured here during the pinning of my Silver Award Ceremony in 2018.

The Art of Friendship is without judgment because it's creative in that it creates a space for you to be just you. I will always love my best friends Lauryn, Lily and Layne Parks. They are my sisters.

At the age of 7, my mom and I co-wrote my first music cd entitled It Doesn't Matter. The song is about encouraging you to continue to believe in yourself even if bullies try to discourage you. This was my very first empowerment project.

When I began hosting The Girls SO Positive show, I had the most amazing guest to come and discuss topics that interest tweens. My two friends Mackenzie Sherry and Rachel Fields were very instrumental in ensuring that we had a great time while filming the show.

I will NEVER forget this day. My grandfather and father were training me how to run to increase my endurance before I joined Girls on the Run.

I was considered borderline overweight when I was 6 years old. By the age of 8, I decided to make working out and making good food choices a part of my lifestyle.

Nick Cottone, who is the Principal at Seneca Ridge Middle School has been very supportive of me during this project.

My first business mentor through the Young Entrepreneur's Academy, Carole Stizza. I have gained so much insight and knowledge from my experience with my mentor.

I'll never forget the day when I met Mrs. Nahid Haidari, M. Ed., Vice Principal, Potowmack Elementary School. After I shared my vision to bring my new So Positive Initiative to her school, she was supportive. Our common thread is that we shared the same passion for building self-confidence in kids.

Brandon G. Wolfe, Ed.D., Principal, Potomac Falls High School is another example of a leader who cares about the students at our school. Dr. Wolfe has supported my ideas from the first day of school. I've been fortunate to have had a tremendous experience with great school administrators.

My brothers have taught me that laughter and love is all about living.

My family is my base. I know that when I'm with them, I'm loved unconditionally. We're at Hermosa Beach, Ca which is one of my favorite places to visit in California.

My dad introduced me to tennis when I was between 3-4 years old. My fondest memories of him and I on the court was when he would always tell me that I was a champion. I didn't realize it then, but he was building my self-confidence.

I am so thankful for my dad and how he has found many ways to build my self-confidence. One of which has always been during the father/daughter dances. I've always felt like a princess in his eyes.

Part of my development has been through my experience in Girls Scouts. I became a Brownie at the age of 7, and today, as a Senior Girls Scout, I understand the value of community service to others within our communities and abroad. I've made lifelong friends and have obtained a clear understanding of the importance in taking responsibility for your actions. My Girl Scout experience has been a part of the development of my self-confidence.

I will always be thankful for the opportunity to give the commencement address at Lowes Island Elementary School June 2018. It was a humbling experience for me because I know that the words that I say could impact someone to reach their highest potential.

I never expected Mr. Dave Shaffer, Principal, River Bend Middle School, to have been the most amazing middle school principal I could have imagined. My middle school years were filled with so much growth as I developed into a young lady with confidence and security in knowing that I was surrounded by an administrative staff that truly supported me and my dreams. River Bend middle school will always have a special place in my heart.

The Young Entrepreneur's Academy opened doors for us to experience being at a round table with CEO's so that we could see firsthand how they work and run their organizations. When you're able to live your dreams, it's becomes the most amazing experience in the world. Having self-confidence means knowing that you will achieve those dreams that will one day turn into opportunities.

My parents have told me since I was a baby that greatness lives in me and today, it has become a part of by being. I believe that it does and I'm thankful for their confidence in me.

Keba is the kind of dog that makes you feel warm and fuzzy inside.

My father has always reminded me that my grandfather instilled the level of confidence in him that would serve as a source of strength throughout his years of growing up. My dad has in return, done the same for me.

Confidence is something that you'll need in any area of your life. When I'm playing singles with my brother, Shang, I know that the slightest bit of doubt could cost me a point. I know that I am talented enough to win every time. And for the times that I didn't win, I still know that I'm talented enough to win every time. I don't equate losing a game to be a loser. I am a champion. My dad taught us that in everything we do, do it as a champion.

Mr. Sparbanie, Principal of Lowes Island and Mrs. Brooks, Vice Principal invited me to speak at Lowes Island Elementary School Graduation June 2018. This was an unforgettable day. Retired Principal Mr. Shafferman, who was my principal at LIES also attended the graduation.

My first book signing was held at One Loudoun Barnes & Nobel in Virginia. Mrs. Carolyn McCormick was there to supported me, and she even wore the Timeless t-shirt! I will be forever grateful for her support and belief in me.

I admire each of my siblings. Amy, Darius and Desmond have all worked hard in school and I'm so proud of them for obtaining their college degrees. My brother Shang is next in line and then, it's me.

My grandmother and Uncle Don have always told me that I can do anything as long as I am willing to work hard and stay committed. I believed in their wisdom, because I've watched them live by the words that they've always spoken to me.

In August 2018, I founded the So Positive Initiative (SPI) at Potomac Falls High School. SPI mentors 5th grade students to help them understand and develop their self-confidence as they matriculate into middle-school. The high school students that work with SPI have an opportunity to develop their leadership and public speaking skills along with earning volunteer and community service hours for their college applications.

I've always dreamed of being the CEO of my own company. My parents taught me that progress is indeed a process that takes time. Creating confidence is the driving force that will help you achieve your dreams.

NOTES:

_____

_____

_____

_____

_____

_____

_____

_____

_____

_____

_____

_____

_____

_____

_____

_____

_____

_____

_____

_____

NOTES:

_____

_____

_____

_____

_____

_____

_____

_____

_____

_____

_____

_____

_____

_____

_____

_____

_____

_____

_____

_____

NOTES:

_____

_____

_____

_____

_____

_____

_____

_____

_____

_____

_____

_____

_____

_____

_____

_____

_____

_____

_____

_____

NOTES:

_____

_____

_____

_____

_____

_____

_____

_____

_____

_____

_____

_____

_____

_____

_____

_____

_____

_____

_____

_____